Contents By Genre

Fiction

Nonfiction

Art

a dinosaur of a little magazine

Issue 3, Fall 2011

Editor & Founder
John Carr Walker

Associate Editor
Katey Schultz

TRACHODON
PO Box 1468
Saint Helens, OR 97051
editor@trachodon.org
www.trachodon.org
www.cheekteethblog.com

TRACHODON welcomes submissions of fiction and nonfiction during
the months of April-May and October-November and flash fiction year-
round. Poetry is currently by invitation only; poets are free to query with a
bio statement and description of work. Note that essays, articles, profiles,
and other journalistic works should be about craft movements, antiquated
processes, or artisan culture. Nonfiction writers are encouraged to query
first. Fiction may be any style, on any theme or topic. Please read our
expanded guidelines by visiting our website or mailing us a stamped, self-
addressed envelope.

Published twice yearly in paperback and ebook formats by Trachodon
Publishing LLC.

Subscription rate: 2 issues (1 year) $18.
Canadian addresses add $3/issue, other international $6/issue.
Sample Issue $10. Canadian $13. Other international $16.
Ebooks are $4.99 per issue.
Limited backlist available. Please make checks payable to Trachodon
Publishing LLC.
Visit our website for special offers, to place orders, and pay by credit card.

John Carr Walker

Editor's Note: Time and Space

I confess, "Doctor Who" is my latest obsession. Mind, I'm not a big television watcher, and not a dyed-in-the-wool science fiction fan, but now and then a show presents characters and tells a story that has me from the first scene, and before long I want to watch every episode, learn something about every actor, and memorize snips of dialogue to be used in future conversation. (And yes, a conversation with me can be quite trying.) Given that there's nearly fifty years of "Doctor Who," I might be riding this obsession for awhile.

Because the Doctor is funny and serious. Wild and in control. Smart and clever and wise. There's a difference between those three, and not many characters can be them all. Furthermore, the character of the Doctor is complex and conflicted, doing good now because he's *not always done good in the past.*

Developing that sort of personal and psychological baggage is a tricky matter for a writer. Backstory, particularly in smaller forms where the audience's attention span also seems shorter, bogs down with quicksand-like speed. Blocks of the past often wind up subtracting from the story, when the writer's intent is to add something crucial, necessary. We all recognize that an adult character in a short story, whether literary fiction or television episode, has a past that has shaped him and informs his current actions. We instinctually recognize that characters don't live and die at the beginning and end of a story. It's natural enough for a writer to want to include this or that trauma from childhood. We want to explain *why* our character is afraid of flying. We want to show the event that made him this way. Won't the reader want to *know* the reasons?

Sometimes a short story writer can learn a lot from television. After all, a TV writer is working in a tiny box. The story has to fit in a certain amount of time, and scenes are going to be broken by commercial breaks, and exposition must be held to an absolute minimum. Given those constraints, the TV writer has to work obsessively with the matter at hand. That is: Where are we? When is it? How did we get here? Who is involved? What's happening now? How is the next thing going to happen? Even in a show like "Doctor Who," in which all of time and space is available, a writer can't afford to get sidetracked with backstory.

The Doctor is almost one thousand years old. Imagine how dull and impossible an episode would seem if we flashed back to his stiff, controling Time Lord father every time the Doctor met a teenager? Instead, mercifully, we get an image of the past here or there, maybe a line of dialogue to tease us, and then the action moves forward, but with a somewhat deeper sense of character all the same. Meanwhile, we remain solidly grounded in time and space.

In Pete Fromm's "God's TV," we spend a few weeks in one house. In Daniel Pinkerton's "The Littlest Goat" it's a few days in one city. Heather Clitheroe's "Bacillus Anthracis" happens in a single morning. And yet the characters are fully alive, *real* people, carrying baggage, wearing scars, with some fresh wounds being afflicted before our eyes. We *suspect* that there's a long history to each of them, but these writers know how to control time and space to thrilling effect. Enjoy.

Pete Fromm

God's TV

I glance out the window, just a quick score check. Deadlocked in the seventh, a pitchers' duel. I watch the windup, the release. Still topping 95 miles an hour. Which gives Annie considerably less than one second to catch me looking.

"Why don't you just go over and introduce yourself?" she says.

I wipe a smudge off the window glass. "What?"

She laughs. "You're all about the windows now? Hang on, I'll grab a rag. Some Windex. When you're done, you can get after the floors."

I finished putting down the hardwood the same day she told me. Me down on my knees, running my hand over all that beautiful, seamless cherry, admiring myself, her sneaking up behind me, touching my shoulder, whispering, "The bun is in the oven." I twisted around, still on my knees, and she was smiling so wide it looked like it might hurt. I brought my dusty fingertips to her waist, and she nodded. "Home cooking, home skillet," she said. We stayed in a motel the whole time I lay the polyurethane down, an air-out weekend afterward, Annie suddenly scared sick of solvents and fumes. I still dust the floors like it's a job, just to see them shine. You could eat off of them. She tells me I'm nesting.

Now she says, "So? What's the score?"

We used to watch baseball. Both of us. Go out for pizza, a pitcher, a night of it. Playoffs anyway. Bet on outcomes.

"One all," I say. "I was just checking."

"Brian," she says, "you can't go around watching the neighbor's TV."

The neighbor. We don't even know his name. An older guy. Alone. Keeps to himself. Watches a TV the size of a billboard. He moved in while we were living in the motel. The only words we've ever spoken were out in the drive when I was hauling in the polisher. He poked his head out, asked how much for two rooms. He thought I was cleaning carpets. That I was the hired help. He must have been doing some of his own watching the neighbs later, seeing me getting familiar with the woman of the house. Must have fogged up his own side of the window.

If she only knew how often
I stand out here at night, my
bare feet making foggy outlines
on my glassy floors, same as
my breath on the window.
The neighbor apparently
never sleeps. I squeegee away
my breath with the edge
of my palm, and we watch
black and white sitcoms, the
driveway between us, the studs
and sheathing and siding,
sheetrock, insulation and
Tyvek, while down the hall,
Annie sleeps for two, mouth
gaping like a dead person's.
Me, I can barely close my eyes
anymore, wondering what our
lives are going to become.

Annie let's me see she's trying not to smile. "You said I'd miss the cable more. Remember?"

"But it's like living next to a drive-in." I wave my hand toward our windows. His. "I mean, God doesn't have a TV like that."

She does this gawping double take. "God?" she says. "God does *not* watch TV."

We get two stations now. Both snowy, unless I stand holding the rabbit ears, which, now and then, she's asked me to do. We ditched the cable as soon as we knew. She'd insisted. For the kid's sake. When I pointed at her stomach—her so thin it was like concave, an absence of space—pointed out that we didn't exactly have kids yet, there wasn't a lot cute about her look. "We're getting used to it," she said, as if getting used to kids before they're around makes more sense than God watching TV.

If she only knew how often I stand out here at night, my bare feet making foggy outlines on my glassy floors, same as my breath on the window. The neighbor apparently never sleeps. I squeegee away my breath with the edge of my palm, and we watch black and white sitcoms, the driveway between us, the studs and sheathing and siding, sheetrock, insulation and Tyvek, while down the hall, Annie sleeps for two, mouth gaping like a dead person's. Me, I can barely close my eyes anymore, wondering what our lives are going to become.

"It's the World Series," I say. "You should not have to buy cable to watch the World Series. FOX. Those assholes. It's like we woke up in a communist country."

"Communists watch the World Series?"

"Hello? Can you say, Cuba?"

She reaches up, does this theatrical push shut of her mouth. She pats her belly. This far along, she looks like a rope knotted in the middle. "I am so sorry, sweetie pie," she says down to her knot. "Your father is a cross you'll have to bear."

"*Without* the distraction of cable," I say, bending low to talk to the knot too, loud enough it'll hear.

"Or the neighbor's TV," she adds.

"Kid won't have a chance."

"This kid," she says, "will have more chances than any TV could ever give her."

"Not God's TV."

"Ass," she says.

"Sticks and stones," I answer.

We look at each other. I say, "You said, *her*."

She shrugs, smiles that way she does now, like she's got a friend with her, the two of them sympathizing, commiserating. I mentioned it once, told her it half gave me the creeps, and she just smiled exactly the same way, said, "You'll get used it. You're adaptable that way." I did my best to take it as a compliment.

"You said I couldn't call it, *him*."

"*It?*"

Walked right into that one. I point again at her belly, like it's the only thing in the room, and say, "Size of that monkey's fist, I'm putting my money on twins anyway. There'll be a her *and* a him."

"Monkey's fist?"

"It's a knot. A big knob to throw a line with."

She shakes her head. Does that protective little belly pat thing that goes hand in hand with the shared smile. "Twins? I don't think so. We were lucky enough to squeeze the one out of you." She turns for the kitchen.

"What is that?" I say after her. "Some sort of size crack?"

"Men," she answers. "Always about their penises."

"You would be too," I shout. "If you had one."

She apologizes to the baby again, for me. She's got more endearing habits.

In the kitchen I find her sterilizing jars. I'm not kidding. She's got some contraption on the counter, like those lazy Susans for poker chips. From the door, I say, "What now?"

"It's a yogurt maker. No hormones this way. No added sugar."

"You can make yogurt?"

"It doesn't come like that from the cow."

I watch her line up the jars, pour in our suddenly organic milk, some powder, magic dust, whatever it is. "Really, Annie. Yogurt?"

"It'll be good for the baby."

"Won't it be a little, I don't know, green, by then?" We've got months left to us.

"I'm just testing it. Learning how."

Great. I know exactly who the guinea pig in this experiment will be. Yogurt. I mean, look at it. "You know, Annie," I say. "This thing, having a baby—"

She turns from her yogurt. *"This thing?"*

I plow on. "I don't think it's something you can train for, be all set up to take like it won't change everything."

"You can try," she says, and, good god, she's shaking like a leaf.

"Annie?"

"You can help," she says. "You could."

"Annie," I say again, and then again. "This baby, it'll teach us whatever we need to know."

"*It?*" she says, and wipes her nose with the cuff of her sleeve, gives a shake of her head exactly like her smile. I wonder, was it always part of the plan, the two of them ganging up on me this way?

She turns back to her yogurt, wipes at her eyes, and I step up behind her, put my arms around her. "It's going to be okay, Annie. Really."

"Hormones," she says. "God, I hate them," but she laughs, a little, and I rub my hand across her belly the same way she does.

"This will be the best monkey fist in the history of knots."

She nods, says, "Considering the father, it's got a chance."

I have no idea how to take that, but we leave it, and just like I knew I would, I eat all the yogurt. I survive.

At the seventh month, just the routine checkup, they catch something a bit off, Annie's exhaustion something to do with her heart, their hearts. They say it's nothing serious, but that they'd like her on bed rest till the big day. Nothing serious? Their hearts? I'm too rattled to catch all the details, but I should know something's up just the way Annie blows it off, tells me it's nothing, that she's excited, that she was made for bed rest. It's a total lie. It's then we start calling it D-day. Yes, as in the invasion. Who knows what we were thinking?

I do what I can. Bring movies home by the cart full, cook, though I don't make her any yogurt. We've never been the stare-all-moon-eyed-at-each-other type, but, leaving for work every morning gets to be a tough kind of thing. I get home as soon as I can, my partner helping where possible, but we've landed the city contract, two new parks to landscape, and there's only so much he can do. I coast up the drive, in case she's asleep, which she sometimes is, turn the key like something might detonate with one false move.

Toeing out of my work boots on the mat, I step inside, don't quite shut the door behind me. If she's not asleep, I usually find her sitting on the couch, or getting something for dinner, which I get after her about, doctor's orders, to which she answers, "Do you have any idea what it's like staring at these walls all day?"

Pretty much the same as it's going to be once this baby's born, I almost say, except for the puking and the pooping and the crying. But I think first, say, "We could get cable again. So you'd have something to do."

"You do know she can hear in there? That she'll come out already knowing our voices?"

"You could watch Sesame Street."

"This child is not going to enter the world thinking Grover is her father."

I don't know how to answer that one, and in the gap she throws in, "She'll have the rest of her life to wish for that."

I tell you, it wasn't always this way. Instead of counting to ten, I say 'hormones' to myself a few times, till the danger is past. "Watch the neighbor's TV then. No sound. She can't *see* out of there."

She stares at me.

"Can she?"

"Yeah, she's got a spy hole in my belly button."

I nod, say, "Cool," then, "Do you feel like anything in particular for dinner?" Some days she does, and I'll get all after it, but then the smell will hit her wrong, or even just the look. One night it was halibut, and, I mean, you can't do much wrong with halibut, but she takes one peek and says, "I'm sorry, I can't do white."

"White?"

"A white meal. No way."

There's rice too, I'll give her that. She leaves the room before the starkness of it all makes her throw up. It's a little too like those ancient sitcoms I watch at night, the husband—that guy always tripping over the ottoman—getting sent out in the middle of the night for pickles and ice cream. It's funnier on TV. Even without sound. I finish both plates. Eating for two.

We're only a couple weeks till D-day when I sneak in from work the way I do, and catch her standing staring out the window. No idea I'm there. I think of taking up cat burglary. I just stand and watch her there by the window, this wife of mine, covered in light, our international life of crime unfolding before me, the childless life we could have had in Monte Carlo, the Riviera, all those James Bond places. Jewels and highballs, tuxedos and gowns.

She's way past monkey-fist now, the baby coiled like a spring inside her, just along for the ride, killing time, sucking her thumb probably, clueless, no idea what waits in store for her out here. That kind of ignorance, she's got to be mine.

Not that there's any doubt of that. That's not what I mean.

Instead of rubbing her belly anymore, Annie's new stance, when she's able to be up at all, is with an arm reached behind her, fist shoved into the small of her back, like there's not one thing about this that was ever comfortable. She's like that now, staring out the window, like she didn't even see me pull in.

It takes me that long to realize what it is she's doing.

"What's on?" I say.

"Baseball," she answers, without so much as a flinch.

"In March?"

"You can get anything on cable. The neighb even watches spring training."

I want to say, "You should see what we watch at night," but I shut my mouth.

"What are you doing home so early?" she asks.

It's maybe the first hint that I've caught her at something she'd just as soon not have me catch her at. "Just lunch," I say.

"We're breaking ground on the river park I was telling—"

"Brian," she says, and that flat and formal, it stops me cold. "You all right?"

She shakes her head. "My water broke."

"What?" I spread my feet a little for balance. "When?"

"About the time you were sneaking in from the garage."

My life as a cat burglar flashes away. "Why didn't you say something?"

She shrugs, still standing there, not once turning to look at me.

All I can do is watch her. "Close game?" I say.

She does that little shrug again, not smiling, then takes this big wavery breath. "I was just, just…"

"Just what, Annie?"

"Just standing here. You know, kind of taking it in. The way things still are right now."

I admit, I look around the room then at myself. All our old stuff in its usual places, even Annie not insisting on total house-proofing yet. "It'll be months before she can crawl," she said. And the word crawl took her to wondering about putting down carpets. Over my floors.

Annie draws in a sudden, sharp breath, digs her fist in harder, reaches out her other hand, fingertips clutching the window sash. And that fast, I nearly am that hapless black and white guy leaping out of bed in his jacket and tie, slapping on his porkpie hat, dashing around the room in circles, that ottoman always out there in his future.

But, after that first quick step toward her, I stop myself, because finally what I see is how exactly that guy I really am, hardly more than a punch line anymore in this house we built together. This is her call now, and I'll move when she does.

Which she does just then, her head hunched forward a little, but turning to look at me, peeking over the length of her arm still holding onto the window sash, the lock there I guess we'll start using now.

"That was a good one," she says.

"You want to go?"

She nods, but says, "I should change. I'm kind of a mess."

"You're fine. Really. Better than fine."

"My pants are soaked," she says, and I realize I'm already behind the curve.

"Of course. Here, I'll get you another pair."

"I think I'll take a shower first."

I give her a look that makes her smile, and she says, "I'm okay, home skillet. This isn't even early innings yet. Barely the National Anthem."

She walks past me toward the shower, just touching my wrist as she goes by. On the gleaming cherry planks beneath the window, I see the little puddle, and I say, "Play ball."

"What?" she shouts. I hear the water gush down. She never remembers to close the door, then always bitches about the draft.

"Nothing," I say, and start down the hall to watch her shower. I'll close the door. I'll pull back the curtain, and she'll smile. I'll lean against the sink counter, seeing her this way one last time, so big and, well, goofy looking, a way it now seems she's always looked, the skin drum tight across her belly, the belly button that embarrasses her now, her used-to-be perfect little inny. "It's just from the spy hole," I told her once, and got a shot upside the head for it.

And when we come back, with her, or him, not it, it'll take months before I remember we have a neighbor, or that he has a TV. God's, as a matter of fact. We'll be the gods then. And gods, as Annie has said, have no use for TV.

Heather Clitheroe

Bacillus Anthracis

This morning I got on the train and I sat down, and I wondered if I loved my husband anymore. Or if he loved me. And then I looked out the window and watched the row houses racing by, and then you got on three stops later. I see you all the time on the train. We both have a habit of choosing the last car. I get on at Perth Street, where the panhandlers loiter about the platform, asking for change and cigarettes, where the newsstand is always open at six in the morning but closed by five. It's a three block walk from my apartment, a part of the city once trendy but now a collection of potholed streets and noodle houses. It's not the best we could get, but it's home. You? Three stops later, closer to what the guidebooks would euphemistically call the market district, where there are silk-screened banners flying from the lamp posts, and where sleepy-eyed teenagers pile on to make the crosstown commute to private school. The both of us get on, take a seat, and settle back—we're used to our routines. We have our passes in the outer pocket of our coats in case the transit police ask to see it. We do this five times a week, you and I, moving one direction in the morning, and another in the evening. We're like clockwork. I observe you as I observe bacteria: I take note of your habits, of your environmental preferences, and I think about whether there is deviation from the pattern of the day before.

You chew your nails. Consistently. Today you're tapping a pencil against your teeth, and putting fingers in your mouth. If

David—David, that's my husband—if he were here, he might smile at you, or even make a comment about the crossword. He likes to talk to people. You know that expression…making friends wherever you go? He strikes up conversations all over the place, perfectly at ease and always with an appropriate joke —not creepy, or racist, or…or…*religionist*. I can't do that. I take the train every day, sit quietly and look out the window. Even the deaf people with those little cards leave me alone.

And here you are, chewing your nails and concentrating on the puzzle. Every day. You just sit down, you take out your folded up back page from the newspaper, and you go to work on the crossword puzzle. If I were David, I might say hello. But then I would want to educate you on the many dangers of opportunistic infections. I would ask you questions. Do you have recurrent bouts of strep throat? Have you ever wondered why?

David tells me that most people don't think about things like this, that they don't count the rows of seats in an airplane to know where the emergency exit would be, or to know the patterns of the behavior of strangers so well. He glances at people and looks away, their habits barely registering with him. Serial killer? No. Purse snatcher? No. Okay, then. It must be some technique of self-preservation, a cheery nod to an ancestral brain that lets him ignore such things. He walks past all the garbage and the gobs of chewed up gum. He sees architectural details and those historical plaques, and he stops to look at them, but in a month he's forgotten and has to look again. He hears the conversations people have, but I just hear traffic and car alarms. I don't live in the city because I like it. The lab is here, and the university, and, so, here I am. And David is here.

Maybe I should have thought about David first. David is here. And so am I. So I am, too.

David feels more at home when he's jostling for space on the train; he grew up in a doorman-equipped building in the heart of the city. He was one of those small children you see led about town by the hand, a backpack hanging off his shoulders and crammed with composition books and pencil crayons. The crowds don't bother him. The press of people all around isn't upsetting, and the smell of various deodorants and perfumes doesn't alarm him. He doesn't notice people with their fingers in their mouths. You can't chew your nails, I say to him. Not in public. Not even at home. Fingers touch everything, and there's bacteria lurking on the surface of that everything. Everywhere. Then it multiplies, grows and spreads, and grows again. Why would you put that in your mouth? Isn't bad language enough?

And let's not even start on *streptococcus*, I would tell him. When I was an undergrad, we stared at so many slides of it that I could draw a picture in my sleep. An ovoid prokaryotic bacteria, gram positive: a small round cell with no nucleus. It can hold a stain solution and show up on a slide, empurpled and proudly declaring to the world: I can give you tonsillitis! I can give you a chest infection that will make you cough until you vomit! A perfectly adapted life cycle for a perfectly adapted bacteria. It's people who chew their nails in public that bear the brunt of droplet transmission illness and bacterial infections, and yet the posters on the inside of the train, the ones printed up by the public health department, they have no effect. People with poor hygiene habits might glance up and take it in, they still get sick, and then they still spread it around for more of the nail-biters to pick it up. I've observed you—yes, you—reading the latest poster on influenza prevention, but still you cough into your hand and not into the crook of your arm, and still you absently-mindedly chew your nails.

It's just…dirty. David tolerates my lectures, but I think he's secretly amused by my fears of bacterial contamination. Sometimes I think he laughs about it with his friends, on those evenings when he goes out for beer with the guys. Last night he came home with those wipes in a plastic bottle—the kind to be used once and thrown away. We'd had a fight…something small.

If I say it was over something unimportant, something small, it makes it seem like we're basically normal, right? So after we had that same fight about why I can't have a little green kitchen sponge, he brought home antibacterial wipes for me. He knows better than to bring flowers.

He understands why I do it: why I wash my hands while mentally singing the alphabet, not stopping until I get to the end. Why I always cut chicken on plastic boards. Why the meat thermometer is always handy. And bean sprouts? Never. These days, we don't even eat that pre-cut salad from a bag…because who knows if it's riddled with bacteria or not? No spinach salads at our table. No cases of *e.coli*, either.

So when David came home and he tossed the bottle of a new kind of germicidal wipes onto the couch, I got a little choked up. Every now and again, he just gets it, and I stop worrying about what he tells his mother or why she stays in a hotel when she visits instead of staying with us in the spare bedroom. He sees it my way: he has a glimpse, maybe…if only for the briefest moment, of the microscopic jungle. It's full of lepers and strains and globules. So few people truly understand

—they think people like me are just compulsive hand washers who need a little positive self talk. Universal precautions spell out exactly how to wash: under the nails, then the fingers, palms, and wrists. It's not something you just pick up. You learn how to do it, and you do it right or you might as well not bother. There's a fine balance to be achieved—one which inhibits the spread of resistant strains of infection while allowing for a bit of friendly flora and fauna to persist. The give and take, as it were, of the natural world. It takes some, but it gives some. It gave me David.

He understands why I do it: why I wash my hands while mentally singing the alphabet, not stopping until I get to the end. Why I always cut chicken on plastic boards. Why the meat thermometer is always handy. And bean sprouts? Never. These days, we don't even eat that pre-cut salad from a bag...because who knows if it's riddled with bacteria or not? No spinach salads at our table. No cases of *e.coli*, either.

We don't have kids. Not yet. The post-doc research program is too intensive, and if I got pregnant, I'd be worried about exposing the fetus to chemicals in the lab and having a baby with flippers for hands. It's probably for the best. Children are always sick. If they're not picking their noses, they're sucking their thumbs, sharing their drink boxes, and eating dirt. It's just the way they are. From a biological perspective, it makes sense to get all of that out of the way during childhood—even I can appreciate that. They're busily building up the immunity needed later on; each childhood disease saves them from dangerous bouts in their twenties, when chicken pox can kill. When life becomes harder to handle. When our new neighbour started teaching first grade, four months ago, she was always sick. David and I used to leave her containers of homemade soup. Poor Angie, we'd say. We liked her, because she told us funny stories of the nosepickers and their high-strung mothers. We thought she was cute, wandering down to check her mailbox in flannel pajama pants and t-shirts with ironical cartoons pictures.

She has a more interesting job than me, I suppose, what with the stories and the jokes. I think that's why David likes to talk to her about her day when they meet in the hallway. He used to ask me about mine, but eventually stopped. I couldn't blame him. When the lab went high security, he was worried. I wasn't sure if it was so much that he was concerned for me, or if he had visions of bioterrorists breaking in and unleashing the plague that spawns a horde of angry zombies—we saw that in a movie. My security clearance scares him. He doesn't like to know that I had to be vetted to be allowed to work in the lab, that there was an interview with a psychologist and a background check. He doesn't like to know that we sometimes get called in to consult for the military.

Angie asked me about my work. Once. We'd stopped to talk in the hallway, me with my briefcase full of papers and lecture notes, and her with a laundry basket stuffed with her unmentionables. I tried to explain. About how a perfect slide would give you images of cells, and how we used to stain and stain, and then peer at images of *Bacillus anthracis*. She gave me a big smile and said something about it being a gift—loving my work and all. The next day, I brought home a glossy photograph of *B. anthracis*. It was a great shot—one of the best ones I'd ever taken, and which was going to be published in the tenth revised edition of *Theories of Cell-Mediated Immunity*. I showed it to her, and she gave me a big smile and said something about 'great job!' But I think it made her uncomfortable, because the smile slid off her face when I told her what it was. Anthrax has a way of doing that. Or maybe it's just me.

That was in September. By October, she wasn't stopping to talk to me. Not really. So she was uncomfortable. So what? By Thanksgiving, I was starting to suspect that she was carrying on with David. I didn't wear pink flannel, and after I found pink fluff on my couch, I had my suspicions. I was certain that the Easter bunny hadn't paid us an early visit. Angie was the type to wear pink flannel pajamas. Not me. Neighborly love should only go so far, and if she'd been on my couch in her flannel, it had gone far enough. Later that week, I found hot pink flannel fuzz in the bathroom. And in the bedroom. It was like an infection in my apartment, quickly spreading from limb to trunk, tendrils stretching towards the internal organs. Angie was the pathogen.

David wasn't entirely to blame. It's a complicated relationship, I told myself. It was partly my fault for working so many evenings and flying off to conferences and poster sessions. His guilt was of a lesser, more benign degree. I could have switched labs and gone to work on Dr. Olafson's toxic household mold project, could have given up the theoretical work we were doing on detecting and neutralizing weaponized pathogens. Could have switched my hours in the lab or come home early a few times just to see if I might walk in on something. I didn't. Angie could have kept her vagina to herself. She didn't do that, either.

It didn't take David long to confess—he did it even before Christmas was upon us. The holiday specials were getting to him, I think—the scenes of loving families and roasting turkeys did not include an adulterous encounter with the next door neighbour. He has an overdeveloped sense of virtue, I suppose, and it fell prey to tidings of comfort and joy. He can lie and cheat, but he can't keep it secret. It's his weakness. He told me how it happened. He was working hard, studying up on the socio-political trends of inner city urban youth and writing his papers, volunteering at the youth center during the day, and I wasn't around in the evenings to talk to. He was lonely. He wanted me to read his work, but I was describing cell-mediated immunity to undergraduates in the mornings and working in the vaccine lab until ten or eleven at night. Angie spent her day singing songs and reading aloud, and when school was out, so was she. She had the time for him. I didn't.

We fought about it. The transgression. I can't help it—I pick at it like a scab when he brings up something I don't want to talk about. Want to have a baby? *You slept with Angie. Won't clean the bathroom? Remember Angie? We shouldn't bother rinsing dishes in a dilute mixture of bleach and water? And you want to have sex? Do I even need to say it?*

Last night, we started arguing about little green kitchen sponges. Again. I couldn't help it. I was ready to have another gnaw on that tired old bone, and he yelled at me to stop. Then he started talking about how I was getting a little crazy with the whole germ thing, and he was sick of it, and everybody in the fucking world had a fucking kitchen sponge and anyways, if he wanted bean sprouts, he was going to have them, and for that matter, why did he feel like he was doing something wrong when he touched his wife, and by the way, who the hell talked about bacteria like it was some kind of friendly puppy? Then he said it. "Lise, if you fucking keep this up, I'm leaving." And then he said he was going for a walk. By himself.

Are you the type of person that stays in on Saturday nights to watch a movie…the kind of person who makes their own ravioli? And do you use your grandmother's recipe for the noodly bits? I don't know exactly *how* to make ravioli, but maybe you do, and you're biting your nails because instead of working on the six-letter word for cold, and maybe you're thinking about what to bring to a potluck dinner and if you can do the ravioli again. You probably go to those.

He put his coat on slowly, and I sat on the couch. I think he was trying to give me a chance to say no, don't, please-I'm-sorry-and-I-can't-live-without-you. I wanted to pick up the advance reader's copy of *Theories of Cell-Mediated Immunity* from the coffee table and chuck it at his head. But I sat there on the couch, and I heard the door close behind him and the unbearable silence afterwards. It's the end of January, and I'm not sure I'm ready for Valentine's Day. Not yet.

The train ride takes twenty-five minutes, usually, but today it's stalled between stations. We've been here for forty-five minutes. Enough time to observe your habits, and here's what I've noticed: instead of texting somebody or making frantic phone calls, you've been doing your crossword puzzle and chewing your nails. You've been thinking about a six-letter word for "cold." You write slowly. I know this about you. You probably wouldn't be caught dead with somebody like me. Would you sleep with somebody like me? A quick fling, something anonymous? Probably not. I can't say that I would, either.

Are you the type of person that stays in on Saturday nights to watch a movie…the kind of person who makes their own ravioli? And do you use your grandmother's recipe for the noodly bits? I don't know exactly *how* to make ravioli, but maybe you do, and you're biting your nails because instead of working on the six-letter word for cold, and maybe you're thinking about what to bring to a potluck dinner and if you can do the ravioli again. You probably go to those. You probably have friends that come over with a bottle of wine—or better yet, invite you to their place for board games. I bet you don't send last minute emails and text messages that cancel on account of migraines and husband-fucking neighbors.

When David said he was going for a walk, I think I must have still been dazed. I didn't run to him and beg him to stay, or offer him kitchen sponges and bean sprouts. I sat there, with my hands folded in my lap, thinking about you, and how most people would see a picture of *Bacillus cereus* and not know it from *Bacillus anthracis*. Do you know the difference? One only gives you abdominal cramping and profuse diarrhea. The other is deadly. It's a common mistake; the untrained eye looks for landmarks, and the mind fills in the details. It's like the difference between smiling at the neighbor and having sex with her in my bed. The undergrads have a hard time with it—the bacteria, that is—but the principle is basically the same. You start off with a slide, thinking you're looking an innocuous and inoffensive thing. But instead you find that you're staring at something deadly. You sit at a lab bench, your neck feeling stiff and your eyes getting jumpy, and you look and look and look. When you finally see it for the first time, you feel a tiny thrill of fear and alarm. Sometimes I hear the undergrads murmur to themselves before they tell their lab partners. *Like, is that it?* Sometimes they shiver. Medieval peasants used to dread anthrax. They called it the black bane. I fear it, but now I know to fear hot pink fuzz more.

It would have been entirely like a movie if he'd moved out last night; the kind that comes on late at night in between ads for skin and blemish cream. The movies about brave women who ditch cheating husbands and then try to make it on their own... and fall in love again with a man who is the opposite of the first, and seems entirely unsuitable and casually oblivious. But it's true love—opposites attracting and all that, and the woman learns that the first marriage was a sham...a prelude to something better. But David came back before I could get to thinking about being brave.

When he came home after the fight, two and a half hours later, he had to rattle the doorknob because of the deadbolt, and I had to get up and let him in. He gave me a kiss and threw out the kitchen sponge. And I put away the reader's advance copy of *Theories of Cell-Mediated Immunity* and blew my nose. I washed my hands. And we had dinner. We didn't talk about anything in particular. I didn't even tell him about the slides I'd stained that day or that Dr. Duchamp had discovered yoga, and that Dr. Olafson wanted to take me to lunch to talk about his a grant proposal and show me pictures of his granddaughter. I didn't tell him about what I'd seen on the train that day, about how you and I are always on the same train car, and how you chew your nails and I wish I could say something to you about the spread of infection.

And he sat and ate his dinner. And I pulled myself together and I ate, too. And we went to bed. We didn't talk but we didn't fight. We had sex, and it was nice but not great. Just two people who hold firm to the familiarity that comes with living together for five years and knowing what to do and how to do it, and an unspoken agreement to do it in the middle of the bed so that neither one sleeps in a damp patch. It was a silent initiation of relations, based upon the observed shape of an erection beneath boxer shorts and a reciprocal quickening of a heartbeat, a sudden flush of arousal. There was a knowledge that satisfaction was at hand and obtainable, the shutting out of an unspoken thought about whether she did it like this, too, and if she had ever considered the optimal angle for penetration as I had, or if she observed the shallow breathing and noises David makes that heralds movement towards climax. I tried not to think about that, but afterwards, lying on my side of the bed in the dark and listening to David breathing, I did. I thought about it.

We didn't talk a lot this morning, either, except to comment on the weather and how the water in the shower was only lukewarm. And I walked three blocks to the Perth Street Station, and waited to get on the last car and looked to see if you were in your customary seat by the door. I took up a seat behind you, where I could read over your shoulder without it being obvious. And now I'm watching you puzzling over the six-letter word for "cold" and wondering if David still loves me. Or if I've ever loved him.

Wintry. Chilly. Frigid. Arctic. Frozen. Any of those would work.

Marianne Dages

Artist Statement

I live in Philadelphia, Pennsylvania and make books, drawings, and prints under the studio name Huldra Press. The name comes from Scandinavian folklore and describes a woman with a fox's tale who lives in the woods.

Natural history, field guides, Shaker objects, folklore, daydreams, the Arctic, libraries, and children's drawings: these are the things I think about and why my work looks the way it does.

I want to live a life surrounded by interesting objects and it gives me great pleasure to make them for others as well.

Foxoxo
2009 12" x 9"
Book page, gouache, pencil, acrylic

King Bird
2008 12" x 9"
Book page, gouache, pencil, acrylic

ago experiments were made at the Rege...ogical Gardens to ascertain if there were an... ...r the old legends that wolves feared the ... ...d instruments such as the violin. Every... ...the story of th... fiddler pursued by ... overtook him he broke a... that the sudden noise of the parting... ...ck to stand... minute, and so enabled him... ...h a tree... ...ch he climbed. Further, that when ... ...h...se given, and played his fiddle, ...ill...when ...apt up ...trie... ...him... ...erimen... ...the Zoo ...ch... ...a there w... no do... ...atev... that ...chord... ...y... ...use the ...ll...rope... ...ve...

INDIAN WOLF

This photograph shows the Indian wolf alarmed. It has a ... reputation for stealing children as well as killing cattle

first sound the wolf began to tremble... uneasily across its den. As the sound gr... and showed such physical evidence of being... that the experiment might be discontinued, or t... wolf is described in "Life at the Zoo" as ha...

...drew ...bac... ...e wh... teeth... ...ss... gums w...how... It... silent t... ...yer approa...ed it; ...e him...ith a ferocious gr... ...ried to seize him.

There are instances of wolves having been quite suc-cessfully tamed, and develop-ing great affection for their owners. They are certainly more dog-like than any fox; yet even the fox has been tamed so far as to become a domesticated animal for the lifetime of one particular indi-vidual. An extraordinary instance of this was lately given in *Country Life*, with a photograph of the fox. It was taken when a cub, and brought up at a large country house with a number of dogs.

WOLF'S HEAD

A very fine study of the head, jaws, and teeth of a female wolf. The head of the male is much larger

Black Wolf
2008 12" x 9"
Book page, gouache, pencil, acrylic

Daniel Pinkerton

The Littlest Goat

Just shy of the Minnesota line they planned to stop so Jonathan could switch places with his daughter. He would swallow another Klonopin, put on his noise-blocking headphones, occupy himself with the book on tape he'd borrowed from the library, and if still awake in half an hour he'd don his sleep mask. The intent was avoidance, the back seat a sensory deprivation chamber. "Just focus on keeping yourself calm," Dr. Chang, at $130 per hour, had reminded him. It was the same plain advice his father had given free of charge thirty years ago.

Jonathan woke to his knee being nudged. The book had ended, he was wearing his mask and headphones and could hear nothing but strangled quietude, the sound of windblown sagebrush. He climbed from the car, stepping foot onto Wisconsin soil. Noreen was hugging her mother on the lawn while Annie embraced Noreen's father. Jonathan hung back until Noreen's father stepped forward to acknowledge him. "Hey, Kent," Jonathan said. The yard was decorated with thorny plants and drooping flowers, each artifact of nature circumscribed by landscape timbers, swimming in white rock. Up near the door a terracotta boy in a sombrero stood beside his burro, and over near the driveway a gazing ball on a pedestal reflected the yard to itself.

"How are things?" Kent asked. His beard, the pipe into which he tamped Middleton's Cherry Blend, something in the timbre of his voice called to mind a college professor, though in actuality he was a landlord, owner of a couple small apartment houses, a car wash, a stake in a local golf course. He appeared to spend his days tinkering with garbage disposals and leaky shower heads and emptying quarters from the carwash lockboxes.

Noreen's younger brother, Steve, and his wife, Kathy, stepped out to greet them, then everyone went indoors to escape the heat. The afternoon spread out in a languid loop of conversation, topics ranging from softball tournaments and mole removals to glaucoma surgeries and the price of soy milk.

Cousins arrived, the house filling with relatives Jonathan vaguely knew. With dinner, some wine for the women, beer for the men. Kent, to everyone's amusement, had joined an ale of the month club. A few people asked about the drive and Jonathan looked for some sign they were probing for details of his condition, which he felt defensive about even after all these years. He answered that the trip went fine and left it at that.

Cousins arrived, the house filling with relatives Jonathan vaguely knew. With dinner, some wine for the women, beer for the men. Kent, to everyone's amusement, had joined an ale of the month club. A few people asked about the drive and Jonathan looked for some sign they were probing for details of his condition, which he felt defensive about even after all these years. He answered that the trip went fine and left it at that.

Eventually he went to look for Annie, who like her father had a tendency, nearly a craving, for solitude. Sure enough Jonathan found her watching TV in the vacant downstairs den. The brown-paneled room, with its drop ceiling and little bubbled windows like the portals of a ship, smelled of dusty wood and subterranean mildew. Strange paintings of children with large dimensionless black eyes hung on the walls. In one corner hummed a green-screened computer on which Kent kept his business accounts. Framed photos lined the Steinway upright in the opposite corner. Though Noreen and Annie were well-represented, Jonathan was amused to find only one snapshot of himself, taken years ago, in which he held his young daughter, his expression indifferent, gaze directed off-camera. He'd been an unintended side effect of a lens aimed at Annie.

Glancing at the TV, he felt a bilious flicker of fear rise in his throat. "Hey, Kid," he said, sitting down fast, the room tilting. "What are you watching?"

Annie changed the channel. "Nothing."

"Turn back to what you had on before."

"You don't want to watch that, Dad. It's just some stupid hidden camera show."

"Turn back."

Annie sighed and for a moment did nothing. Then she placed the remote on the end table and left the room, bounding up the stairs.

He wasn't wrong about what he'd glimpsed: the collapse of a major bridge, the I-35 in the midst of a Minneapolis rush hour, a high-traffic interstate span over the Mississippi. It could've been the I-94 as easily as the I-35—could've been Jonathan and his family who felt themselves floating in that fractional instant as steel and concrete gave way beneath and they were deposited into a churning river.

He felt the nausea coming and was at least able to push himself up, reaching the laundry room utility sink before disgorging the ales of the month he'd drunk. It took weeks for Jonathan to prepare for these annual voyages to the in-laws' that carried him over the I-94—extra sessions with Dr. Chang, visualization and deep-breathing exercises, motivational CDs—and now for something like this to happen. Even without consulting Chang, Jonathan knew it was a setback. At least after vomiting he felt a little better, drinking water from the faucet, sprinkling some detergent flakes into the basin and scrubbing away the unpleasant smell before returning to his seat on the couch.

He heard footsteps on the stairs but couldn't draw himself

from the TV. Apparently Annie had gone for reinforcements. Noreen touched Jonathan's neck, then her arms were linked over his chest as she bent to speak into his ear. "Why don't you come upstairs and be sociable," she said.

"In a minute," Jonathan muttered. His new mental exercise, try as he might to suppress it, was envisioning himself in one of those rush hour vehicles. A sourceless rumble, the car ahead of his vanishing, the hollow sweeping uplift in his stomach as he plummeted. There and then not there, the magician's cape lifted away to reveal, *voila*, nothingness.

"Honey, it's not healthy for you to watch that."

"I need to see what happened."

"You can read about it in the paper," Noreen said. "Come be with your family. Annie's worried about you." But Annie was always worried about one thing or another, always cautious, slow to smile. He remembered the story she had requested over and over as a child. *On the way up was a bridge over a cascading stream they had to cross; and under the bridge lived a great ugly troll, with eyes as big as saucers, and a nose as long as a poker.* Annie seemed indifferent to the fate of the billy goats but wanted to know every detail about the troll. What language did it speak? Did it have a name? Had it come from a long line of trolls?

Jonathan imagined that even at age four Annie recognized, if dimly, her father's fears and was mirroring them. She knew he went each month to visit a doctor but that this doctor did not give vaccinations or stitch wounds or even look in people's ears. She knew that for some reason all car trips must be diligently plotted in advance. She knew that the amber pill vial on the high bathroom shelf was regularly drained and replenished by her father. Jonathan wondered if she thought it was the trolls under the bridges rather than the bridges themselves that frightened him and that this was why she fixated on them.

"Okay," Jonathan said finally, allowing himself to be led upstairs. Yet soon enough he found himself at the far edge of the couch in a living room empty except for the dog that slept pressed against him, emitting a withering sigh with each distension of its tight pink belly. Full of guilt, strange stirrings, Jonathan crept back down. He wasn't sure what drew him to the news reports, only that his desire resembled the almost irrepressible impulse of the acrophobic to step toward the ledge and peer over. He navigated the channels, hungry for new details. When Noreen appeared a second time to collect him, her hand in his hair caused him to start.

"You can't do this," she said, close enough for him to smell the merlot on her breath, an opaque odor of dried blood, snake skins, rain-wet leaves.

"What do you mean?"

"You've been down here for hours."

"What?" In the falsely lit basement, windows curtained, he had failed to notice the daylight giving way to dusk and then nightfall. "Where's everyone at?"

"Steve and Kathy went home, Mom's finishing the dishes, Dad's puttering in the garage. Annie's reading, I think."

"What'd you tell them?"

"That you weren't feeling well."

"Oh." Jonathan resumed flipping channels.

"Are you coming?"

"Pretty soon."

She swung around to face him. "Don't make me wrestle the remote out of your hand."

"I'll be up," Jonathan smiled. "I promise." Then he pulled her toward him and kissed her, their sour breaths meeting.

"What was that for?" Noreen asked. Rolling before Jonathan's eyes were images of oddly-angled rebar jutting from concrete skins like open fractures, a tanker truck in flames, divers entering the floodlit river. Something was being confused here. In murky water he kicked toward the surface without any promise of reaching it or of knowing, even, which way the surface lay. When he went to touch his wife's breast she jerked backward, startled, as though from something trying to strike.

"What are you doing?"

Jonathan reached a second time.

"Stop it," Noreen hissed. The way her eyes rolled back, the wild glance at the stairway, reminded him of a spooked animal.

The bridge had been given a deficiency rating and should've been rebuilt. That's what the experts were saying. Maybe terrorists were involved. "Just come upstairs," Noreen said, leaving Jonathan alone again with the TV. A bus hinged on the precipice like something from a movie, with terrified schoolchildren streaming out the emergency door. It was time for deep breathing, another Klonopin.

•

Later Jonathan couldn't sleep; his mind wouldn't allow it. Seventy wounded, thirty unaccounted for, and this strange bed with its musty sheets fished from the back of the linen closet just prior to their arrival, the scratchy brocaded bedspread, the bridge crumpling like something a kid might build out of popsicle sticks. The sleep mask made no difference. A cricket outside their window sounded as though it had infiltrated their room. Jonathan put on his headphones and tried listening to the story on tape but it made no sense, the characters behaved without motive, saying things to each other that people didn't really say. He tried squeezing his eyes shut until finally they jerked open from the strain. The darkness presented its dangers to him, then his eyes adjusted and the intruder in the far corner became a floor lamp again. Headlights slid across the ceiling, bars of muted slithering light. Jonathan now tried holding his eyes open but they began blinking furiously. If this bridge could collapse, then so could any other. He was the littlest goat crossing timidly, naively, with only the bony frame of his inadequacies to serve him.

Jonathan rose and snuck downstairs, turning the TV on low.

•

"Maybe we ought to call Chang." It was early morning; Noreen wore her baggy gym shorts and oversized t-shirt. The way she hugged her knees to her chest, tugging the t-shirt over them, made her seem suddenly younger, a girl again. There were these fleeting glimpses—painful if only for a moment—of what Jonathan and Noreen had been before the occlusions of adulthood, parenthood, middle age. She had aged well, better than he, and Jonathan faced the sudden realization that she could leave him; Noreen had never given any indication of doing so, yet he thought that in his current state he'd understand if she did.

"I don't want to call Chang," he said.

"Why not?"

"It's not a big deal."

"Look, you need help with this, and I'm not sure I know what to do."

They sat in the kitchen, Noreen at the table, Jonathan on a stool at the center island. He heard footsteps on the floor above and worried Noreen's folks might overhear. "Don't know how or aren't willing?" he said.

"Don't be that way."

"Leave it alone then."

"We're meeting Steve and Kathy for breakfast. Do you feel like going?"

"Of course," Jonathan said, though he didn't. His eyes were performing irritable tricks in their sockets; his stomach felt acidy, wound-up; he had a persistent metallic taste in his mouth. But to beg off would be to surrender. Forward momentum; he had to keep moving. *And then the big billy goat flew at the troll, and poked his eyes out with his horns, and crushed him to bits, body and bones, and tossed him out into the cascade, and after that he went up to the hillside.*

Noreen's folks had chosen a place that served breakfast all

day, with pies displayed in a tiered cooler near the cash drawer and obsolete farming implements cluttering the walls in an effort to work at the patrons' feelings of nostalgia. Jonathan had been to the restaurant before, had stood around while Kent and his wife, Grace, sighed over the pitchfork heads and hay cutters and sickle scythes mounted like museum pieces.

While the group waited to be seated, Jonathan went into the restroom and drank some water from the tap. His tongue was spackled with a curious whitish film that he found he could rake furrows into with his fingernail. Emerging, Jonathan discovered his group gone and wandered in search of them until finally a waitress intercepted him, guiding Jonathan to his table.

"You tie one on last night or what?" said Steve, when Jonathan appeared. Kathy elbowed her husband but failed to dampen his grin.

Everyone crouched behind their menus, and Jonathan, by way of reply, made a stifled sound through his nose intended as a laugh. He once in awhile wished idly that Steve would fall into an abandoned mineshaft. The menus here were like laminated sheets of roofing tin, they had that height and heft to them. It appeared that the specials were named for well-known shipwrecks. The waitresses just looked bewildered, like victims of blunt traumas.

"How's the lending business these days?" Kent asked Noreen.

"Could be better," she said. "People are going to lose their jobs over this subprime stuff."

"Your job's not in danger, is it?" Kent said.

She glanced at Jonathan, who'd been swallowed by his menu. "I don't think so."

"What about you?" Kent asked, turning to Jonathan. "How's your job going?"

Jonathan inched his menu down to look at Kent, registering that the man staring at him was awaiting a response, but he could think only of the victims inside those cars, their final thoughts, whether they lived for any length of time in the frothy, utterly dark water or whether they perished instantly. "I can't believe it happened right at rush hour," Jonathan murmured.

His daughter's face flushed. "What are you having, Grandma?" Annie asked.

Grace took up her glasses and menu. "I think I'll order the *Lusitania*," she said.

"But you don't care for bacon," Kent reminded her.

"Maybe I'll get something on the side."

"I'll take your bacon if you don't want it," Steve said.

"I want cake," said the younger of Steve and Kathy's two children.

"Honey, they don't have cake here," said Kathy.

"I want cake," the boy repeated, adamant.

Jonathan pushed himself from the table and stood. "Excuse me," he said, patting his pockets for the bottle of Klonopin, unable to find it. He thought maybe he'd left the vial in the restroom, but on entering he found the counter empty. An employee stood at the urinal, so Jonathan went into a stall and sat there breathing and counting, his Victorious Breaths, trying not to accuse the kid of theft.

Jonathan heard the toilet, the sink, the hand blower, the give of the door as the employee returned to work. It had never struck him before how overly pressurized these bathroom sounds were—the coursing of water in the basin or bowl, the blast of air through the dryer, the crackling stream of urine striking the porcelain. Jonathan came out of the stall and began sifting through the trashcan. The bottle probably wasn't there, it was probably back at the house at the bottom of his suitcase, but he couldn't keep from searching. A man entered with his young son to find Jonathan hunched over the garbage. Jonathan looked up and tried to smile but the smile seemed malignant on his face, barnacled there. The man turned his son around, herding him out the door.

On exiting, Jonathan found himself facing the displayed pies emitting their mass-produced gleam of perfection, like cigarette packages or kitchen utensils or caskets. A bored hostess leaned on her lectern, texting. Somewhere to his right, beyond view, were in-laws and a daughter and a wife; to his left were the twin sets of entry doors like bulkheads on a submarine. A precise square of white sunlight lay on the carpeting. A coin-op machine stood stork-like on one leg, dispensing Chiclets. Jonathan wandered outdoors, into a morning sun which instantly became an irritant, sending him toward the restaurant's shaded backside. He leaned against the building, drawing a couple more cleansing breaths through his nose. A smell of ripening garbage drifted from the dumpster. The cars parked out back belonged obviously to the help, bumper stickered VWs and wide-tired muscle cars. The heavy rear door opened and a kid appeared with folded boxes tucked under his arm. He dropped them and lit a cigarette before seeing Jonathan.

"Hey," Jonathan said, nodding.

"What's up?" The two of them examined the space behind the restaurant, though there was little to see: a privacy fence flanked with weeds and beyond that the bland posteriors of tract houses. "Are you, um, a homeless person?" the kid asked after a moment.

"No," Jonathan said, jerking his thumb toward the building behind him. "My family's inside."

"Why aren't you?"

"Not hungry." They heard voices, customers leaving the restaurant, car doors slamming. "Did you hear about that bridge collapse in Minneapolis?" Jonathan ventured.

"Uh-uh," said the employee, picking with two fingers at something on the tip of his tongue. Jonathan wasn't sure whether to take his grunt as a yea or nay.

"I can't believe the bridge was in such terrible condition and they let people keep using it."

"Makes you wonder," the teen said, watching the houses with a slight expectant smile as though awaiting, say, a topless woman to begin some trampoline routine, appearing at flickering intervals above the fence line. He dropped his cigarette and extinguished it with his boot. "I've got to take these boxes over," he said, nodding toward the dumpster.

Jonathan watched him go. He thought of his daughter inside, sandwiched between Steve's two brats, head down, hands folded in her lap, skin so translucent you could trace the shadowy greenish-purplish pathways running beneath. She seemed unaccountably frail, yet he and Noreen couldn't coax her outside, couldn't get her into the swimming pool even on a day like this, couldn't get her to don a swimsuit. It had gotten so bad they'd begun writing notes of excuse from swim days in PE. Jonathan didn't much like doing it but was willing to sign off for his daughter's sake. He just hoped his own fears weren't somehow mutating, a virus seeking a new host.

•

When Kent discovered Jonathan standing there in the shade, he acted as though he'd happened onto him by chance while appraising the building's brick facade, its faded signage, the barberries sunk into river rock. "Weren't feeling up to breakfast, huh?" Kent asked.

Jonathan shook his head. As tempting as the *Andrea Gail* sounded—eggs benedict, a short stack of pancakes—he did not feel like eating a shipwreck, not when he feared becoming one.

"I've got some errands to run today," said his father-in-law. "Feel like tagging along?"

"Noreen roped you into trying to get me out of the house?"

Kent smiled. "I'd be lying if I said it wasn't true."

They dropped the others off and switched to Kent's pickup. Masking tape, pliers, and orphaned strands of electrical wire spilled over the seat, pooling on the thinning floorboards, a slight patina of sand or grit coating everything. Jonathan envied this truck. It seemed that the men of his father's generation all had vehicles like these, filled with evidence of the capable work they did with their hands. The fathers seemed far better equipped to fix, improvise, and endure. The biggest billy goats. Kent listened to public radio as he drove, puffing his pipe, bluing the cab with smoke despite the open windows. A commentator discussed the bridge collapse, and Jonathan strained to hear.

The tone of Kent's voice made Jonathan feel he wasn't threatening him, wasn't plotting to dangle his son-in-law by his ankles from the bridge, and the river itself wasn't terribly daunting, Jonathan assured himself, just shallow and slow-moving.

"Confronting your phobia, is that the way to go?" Kent asked, startling him. "Has this doctor you've been seeing, has he mentioned anything about that?"

"That's part of it," Jonathan said. "It's really a multi-dimensional therapy."

"Multi-dimensional?"

They passed the city pool, an elementary school, a row of sturdy little two-bedroom bungalows referred to now as starter homes, purgatories you endured for a few years before escaping to one of the developments at the edge of town. "Listen, Jonathan, I've got some work to do at one of my properties, but we'll have to cross the river to get there. You think that'd be okay?"

The tone of Kent's voice made Jonathan feel he wasn't threatening him, wasn't plotting to dangle his son-in-law by his ankles from the bridge, and the river itself wasn't terribly daunting, Jonathan assured himself, just shallow and slow-moving. This time of year drunken kids drifted down it on inner tubes lashed together, occasionally displaying their nakedness to each other. How treacherous could it be? The biggest risk, it seemed, should the bridge give way and Jonathan find himself waist-deep in torpid water, was contracting something bacterial. Still, the I-35 collapse in the cities had seriously unnerved him, and he needed another pill, something to take the edge off. Jonathan muttered that he thought he could make it across.

When they neared the bridge, traffic increased, carloads of kids pulling into the lots along the launch point, offloading vast two-handled coolers. Jonathan cradled his head in his arms, trying to diminish the pounding in his chest. It shamed him to do so, but he didn't particularly want to freak out in front of his father-in-law either. He recited the numbers he'd committed to memory, like a mantra, the failure rates for bridges, the fatalities, yet now with the collapse in the Twin Cities the numbers were skewed, the rates had increased, he'd need to find some fresh data...

"We're across," Kent said, touching his shoulder.

They reached the apartment house, a two-story brick building of ten or so units with a tiny first floor laundry and a gravel lot with sunken railroad ties to mark the parking spots. Kent lifted some window screens from the pick-up bed, Jonathan grabbed the toolbox, and they entered, the hallway cool, damp, dark as a mushroom farm. Before they reached the tenant's apartment the music reached them, hip-hop loud enough to make the floor vibrate.

The man who answered must've been at least seventy-five, arms striated with ropy muscles, skin loosening into papery folds. He was wearing a ribbed undershirt and Levi's, the exposed skin of his arms and neck crosshatched with green tattoos, courtesy of prison or the Navy or both, ink that had bled over the years until becoming as indecipherable as tea leaves. Wordlessly he opened the door wide enough for them to squeeze through.

"Hi, Don," Kent said.

"Who's this?" Don nodded toward Jonathan, who fought the urge to smile at the old man's defensiveness.

"My son-in-law, Jonathan," Kent said.

Don examined Jonathan the way one might a plumbing leak. "Those loose screens I was telling you about are in here," he said, steering them past the kitchenette, sink blooming with dirty dishes, garbage bags heaped by the fridge. The living area was cluttered and foul smelling, beer and wine bottles on every level surface, some half full, some crammed with cigarette butts, gnats skimming the rims. A box fan turned in the window, breathing sour air into the room, which was stifling, overcast, with a Vietnam POA flag darkening one wall and not much else in the way of adornment. The bedroom Don led them to was more of the same, but with various survival knives, butterfly knives, throwing stars—harmless, cheaply made weapons kids bought at flea markets—scattered around. In fact the entire apartment, tenant included, looked as though a swap meet had stumbled in, evacuated its bowels, and departed. Jonathan hovered in the bedroom doorway, reluctant to enter, while Don and Kent navigated around piles of crumpled shirts, pants, tarnished underpants. Jonathan glimpsed a pair of jungle print bikini briefs and again fought the impulse to smile.

The bed was scattered with the skeletal remains of chicken dinners. It was saddening to think of the man taking his take-out meals alone in the tiny bedroom, idly flicking open his dull flea market blades, maybe cursing the TV, the government, who knew?

"I seen some more of them camel jockeys at the Jonzy Market the other day," Don mentioned as Kent examined the screens. "Seen any around?"

"No, Don, I haven't," Kent said, back turned, still fiddling with the tracks the screens fed into.

"How about you?" he said, addressing Jonathan for the first time, but before he could reply Kent spoke for his son-in-law. "Jonathan doesn't live around here."

"You getting one of them keypad locks for the front door?" Don asked, returning his attention to Kent.

Kent rose, wiping away the sweat over his eyes. "I looked into it, Don, but they're kind of tricky to install. I'll have to give it some more thought."

"Well don't think on it too long," Don said. "I'm getting fearful of my personal security here."

Kent sighed. "Don, I don't really see anything wrong with

these screens."

The tenant eyed the landlord, unsure whether he was serious or not. "If it's all the same," he said finally, "I'd like for you to switch them out anyhow." His voice took on an edge that might've seemed threatening had Jonathan not glimpsed the old man's Saturday night jungle briefs, so it surprised Jonathan that his father-in-law set to work without protest.

"I'm gonna get me a beer," Don said, satisfied that his request was being carried out. "You want one, Kent?"

"No thanks, Don." Some sort of Jamaican reggae-rap droned on the stereo. The stifling heat and dense locker room smell of the apartment made it difficult to breathe, and Jonathan imagined that molds and spores, agents of slow chaos, thrived beneath the visible veneer. He was forced to move out of the doorway so Don could get by, and, faced with Jonathan's proximity, Don was in turn forced to offer him a beer, which Jonathan refused.

"That ought to work," Kent said, gathering up his tools and the old window screens, which to Jonathan appeared identical to the new ones. They were made to wait while Don sniffed at Kent's work, leaning in, feeling along the frames. Meanwhile the lyrics of the song playing on the stereo became so vile, so hateful of women, that Jonathan felt embarrassed hearing them in his father-in-law's presence.

Outside they leaned against the pick-up, gazing into the bed at the objects accumulated there, the spare tire and tire iron, a few crimped Pepsi cans, a couple heavy-duty plumbing wrenches. Sweat shone on Kent's face and he took quick panting Lamaze-style breaths. Jonathan had his own calming breathing routine, so he couldn't really comment. Neither of them spoke. After awhile they climbed up into the pick-up. Kent's hands trembled as he pinched tobacco from its pouch into the bowl of his pipe. Jonathan's instinct was to keep quiet, but he knew he should ask if Kent was alright.

"I'm sorry about that, Jonathan," Kent said. "That guy is a

real nut job. I should've given you fair warning." They pulled out of the lot, back toward Kent's home, toward the Apple River.

"No big deal—"

"He's always pestering me, and when I get over there it's nothing. Loose window screens. I bet I've checked those things five times. I keep switching the same screens back and forth, he doesn't know the difference."

As they neared the river Jonathan felt his chest tightening, a septic hand in there squeezing, but before they could cross, Kent slowed the truck and they pulled in at one of the river entry points, parking alongside a lavender-colored party bus. From here they had an undisturbed view of the water. Around them kids milled with a vacant sort of good cheer, shirtless guys in backwards caps, girls in bikini tops and board shorts holding cans of economical beer. Employees of whatever company had turned this place into whatever it was (part tailgating party, part amusement ride) dispensed inner tubes and made change from inside a Morton building, feeding people to the river.

"You ever done that?" Kent asked, nodding toward some kids wading into the water.

"Tubing? Never have. How about you?"

"Sure. Grace and I used to bring the girls here in the summer." A few yards distant a coed lowered her shorts, revealing a thong bikini to her enthusiastic male companions. "Not so much a family atmosphere anymore," Kent observed dryly, teeth tapping a telegram on the stem of his pipe. "Probably a lot more fun, though—unless, you're not afraid of water?"

"Water doesn't bother me," Jonathan said, "just bridges."

"I didn't want to go in there alone today," Kent said, and at first Jonathan thought he was still talking about tubing. His father-in-law kept an eye on the river. It was a plain thing oozing out of the ground, running a few miles along the channel a glacier had cut before being swallowed by the Mississippi.

"You mean that old guy's apartment?" Jonathan asked finally. "He seems pretty harmless."

"All those weapons laying around? I went in there once and saw a pistol sitting on the table—not some old six-shooter but a nickel-plated thing like you'd see on TV. He does that kind of stuff to intimidate people."

Sweat darkened Jonathan's shirt, and leaning forward he tugged it loose like wet gauze. Kent did not seem inclined to leave. "I bet he's just lonely and paranoid," Jonathan said.

"I keep dwelling on the man who killed those people in Milwaukee and put them in his freezer," Kent said.

"You think Don's got somebody in his freezer?"

"That guy, Dahmer, he lived in an apartment complex. He had neighbors, a landlord. I take these people's rent checks, I give them a place to stay, but I don't know anything about them. That's my point."

"Why not evict him?" As soon as Jonathan said it he realized he was being dismissive. The sleepless night, the medication, the heat, all had conspired to exhaust him. The world was buzzing with tiredness, and he heard and spoke everything through the distortion.

"It's not that easy," Kent said, glancing away. Then he changed the subject. "What about your sessions with the doctor? Have they been fruitful?"

So that explained the hesitations, the detour to this scenic lookout: Kent had been gathering the courage to ask about Chang. "They're fine, I guess," Jonathan said.

"What about the pills you take?"

"Drugs are good." Both of them laughed harder than they should have, and the ensuing stillness seemed denser. Jonathan watched the girl in the skimpy shimmering bikini. She'd pulled her shorts up quickly enough, but she seemed to radiate now with the knowledge she'd awarded those around her, glowing with the afterimage. "Dr. Chang has me write things in a notebook. That seems to help."

"How so?"

"I'm not sure. It helps you organize things in your head."

"Like a diary?" Kent said.

Jonathan winced at the thought of a book locked with a delicate key, hearts and unicorns on the cover. "He has me do breathing exercises too." Thong girl migrated hostess-like from group to group, tossing her head back in laughter to reveal the perspiration gathered along her jugular. She had a deep even tan garlanded by a little shimmering diamond in her navel.

"Breathing exercises," Kent said. "I can feel my breath catching in my chest sometimes. I try to inhale deeply and it just stops midway through."

Jonathan kept up his vigil of the girl. There was the way she touched her right earlobe—only the right, never the left—or the loose-wristed way she handled her beers or the way her flip-flops scuffed along the asphalt as she walked, a habit that in others would've grated but in her became endearing, a rhythmic means of announcing her entry into the next group of people. But once she came to a stop she held still, making Jonathan all the more conscious of his own fluttering nervousness and constant hand movements, his reluctance to look people in the eye. Soon the girl would board her tube and present herself to the sun and the water with a debutante's ease and confidence. She moved with too much surety to ever put herself under threat.

Jonathan, for his part, would return to his underground lair, his dour sofa and closed curtains and television tuned to the latest grisly developments, the craggy pile of riprap from under which he might listen for the clatter of hooves.

Kent reached for the keys.

"You think we could sit here a little while longer?" Jonathan asked.

Kent leaned back, working his pipe, exhaling smoke. "I don't see what it could hurt."

Ray Scanlon

Printer's Devil

Multiplicity has always fascinated me. Show me hundreds or thousands of an item, and I'm mesmerized: a jar of jelly beans, a bin of six-penny nails in the hardware store, a glass-fronted beehive. When I snap out of it, there's the faint lingering sense of order and structure, of a whole greater than the sum of its parts. So it's no surprise that, at a young age, the craft of printing— the technology to make multiple exact clones of an original, albeit paper, seized my mind. Today, any damn fool can write and publish on the Internet, spewing out pages at will on ink jet machines with the click of a mouse. But forty years ago, before cheap, offset printing fast began crowding out letterpress—the One True Printing—printing was an art.

A letterpress page was a thing of beauty, regardless of its typographical competence, printed the way God and Gutenberg intended, on paper temporarily sandwiched between inked type and a hard place. Paper is essentially two-dimensional, unless you're prone to carrying a micrometer, and it gained its rightful third dimension by dint of the impression made by metal type. The metal just kissed the paper—otherwise the type would fast wear out—but the paper was altered in its essence, gaining maybe half a thousandth of an inch in thickness, and a whole new robustness. Embossed words magically became tangible, incarnate. You could see and feel the difference in the paper.

By the time I was ten or so, I desired, with a startling intensity I'd soon recognize as lust, to have the power to print. In grade school I sent away for a cereal-box hectograph, which I probably used to produce right-wing screeds. Then, as a sixth-grade trusty, I was allowed to run the spirit duplicator, which we mistakenly called the Mimeograph. I cranked it and it spit out pastel-not-found-in-nature purple worksheets—it was heaven to sniff the alcohol-dampened paper. Later on during junior high and high school, I became interested in photography (though showing no extraordinary talent for it) and indulged book learning about lithography, etching, engraving, silk screening, and other visual crafts.

It was a welcome balance to a whole school year of unremitting life of the mind, a chance to do physical work, learn manual skills, and produce something palpable. There were rooms full of seductive machines that you could really get your hands on and it was gratifying to learn how to cooperate with them.

As a boy not yet twenty who'd just finished coasting through my freshman year at Worcester Polytechnic Institute full of piss and vinegar, I was hardly past days when the acme of sophisticated wit was to sneer, "Nice play, Shakespeare," at the committer of some teen-age *faux pas*. The world was, in fact, my oyster: possibilities were endless, there was unlimited time, and the concept of lifespan was utterly alien. It was a heady year, 1969. There was an American on the moon, I drank my first illegal beer, and I had a summer job at the Foxboro Company print shop. At last I was a printer, or at least a printer's devil.

The Foxboro Company, a good-sized manufacturer of process control instrumentation, had then been a New York Stock Exchange-listed public corporation for only about ten years. It was still family-run, with a long heritage of benign paternalism. The company was a good neighbor to the town of Foxboro, providing employment and allowing the town to make use of the physical plant when it would do some good (this was before the return-on-asset-driven bean-counters got into the picture). One of its public services was summer jobs for children of employees, and in that summer of 1969 I landed one.

It was a welcome balance to a whole school year of unremitting life of the mind, a chance to do physical work, learn manual skills, and produce something palpable. There were rooms full of seductive machines that you could really get your hands on and it was gratifying to learn how to cooperate with them. I coaxed clean copies out of a Multilith press, even though it's just plain wrong to rely on the immiscibility of oil and water as a basis for printing. I prepared negatives for offset plate-making by retouching pinholes with opaque, and I cranked up our small hand-fed letterpress as fast as it'd go to keep me awake after long nights of pondering the workings of the universe with my friends.

And of course there was plenty of new, esoteric vocabulary to take in. Imagine my prurient delight to learn that Agnes, who taught me retouching, was an "offset stripper." The print shop actually was located on Wall Street in Foxboro, so I'm still able to say with a straight face, in a hoary gem of small talk that's served me for decades, that I used to work on Wall Street with a stripper named Agnes.

There is no way a Linotype could possibly work, but it did. Consider a mutant typewriter on steroids, orders of magnitude more complex than Rube Goldberg's worst nightmare, and think of a sort of self-organizing, spidery intelligence emerging from the seeming chaos of hot lead slugs falling into a galley, surrounded by a myriad of large-postage-stamp-sized brass matrices marching ant-like up and down the machine. I cast type-metal ingots to feed its maw, but I was never allowed to touch the keyboard. I don't think Twilight Zone writers had to stretch far to come up with the episode in which a Linotype under the mephistophelian fingers of Burgess Meredith composed stories that came true when printed in a struggling local newspaper, resulting in massive sales increases. Of course there was a soul at stake, but I leave it as an exercise for the reader to find out what happened. Our print shop Linotype, true to character, also had a diabolical bent: it would squirt molten lead at the operator if he weren't eternally vigilant. I could have watched that machine for hours.

The machines did not run themselves; people were involved. I had to deal with a group of people who, unlike my parents and teachers, were not necessarily devoted heart and soul to my welfare and my social skills were not too finely honed. But I was open to the experience; scraggly, asymmetrical Afro and bell-bottoms notwithstanding (even with an acrid whiff of communist academe about me), I apparently did not present much of a threat to the print shop tribe. At least none of the adult males killed and ate me, and I think several were capable of it...

Dave ran the big Miehle four-color offset press. He was crew cut and graying, powerfully built, active in Boy Scouts and bicycling, and stuttered. We called each other "fascist" and "hippie," just to make sure we understood each other, embracing the epithets for the clarity they brought. We had good talks.

Lawne. I suspect he thrived on the attention commanded by always having to explain: "It's pronounced Lonnie but spelled L-A-W-N-E." He ran a Multilith and spent his spare time taking ballroom dancing lessons to meet women. This model for meeting women has always seemed broken to me; it should be talk, then touch; conversation, then the vertical expression of horizontal thoughts. My own dancing lessons, taken under compulsion in eighth grade and later in the waning days of my first marriage, only reinforced this notion.

Gus asked me what I was studying at school and when I told him I was a math major, he admitted that fractions had always stumped him. He was a simple man, given to expressions of lechery when female pulchritude appeared, as blatant and obvious as a cartoon character with eyeballs bugging out. It was comical to watch, downright creepy if you were on the receiving end—ask my sister who worked at the print shop a couple years later.

Tommy was an older Irishman, indoor-pale, with a shy smile, reputed to be drunk twenty-four/seven. He worked in the bindery, where the massive shears had a safety interlock you had to physically span with both arms spread wide. This prevented inadvertent hand-chopping, but I suspect a determined suicide might have been able to behead himself.

Danny was soft-spoken and friendly, though often he talked to us as if we were backward children. This was, no doubt, a side effect of coaching the worst team in the Foxboro Company softball league, where it was probably the only way he could maintain his sanity while dealing with players who didn't have the wherewithal to play even minimally adequate ball. Other teams seemed composed exclusively of fit young men who'd spurned semi-pro contracts just so they could play for the Foxboro Company. Our team had a couple of those, but Tommy and I more than neutralized them. Yes, I played, though athletically incompetent and uninterested in sports: Danny cajoled me into it. He was so desperate for enough warm bodies to field a team that it wasn't even a question of "trying out."

John was a Linotype operator. Linotype operators, like their machines, are a breed apart. He smoked Parodis at the keyboard, had a wide-ranging curiosity, was independent possibly to a fault, and a mean conversationalist. He'd draw me out on any number of topics, and then draw me in, green young whippersnapper with no experience of life whatsoever, until I was irretrievably far out on a limb. Every few years I bump into him in Attleboro, and it's still a pleasure to converse.

The print shop turned out to be a useful laboratory for engaging in the proper study of mankind, and it was high time I started to learn how to be a rudimentary social human. The print shop was also, much more obviously, a lab in which to study work, another cornerstone of humanness. Even in my short tenure as a novice printer I could discern a hierarchy of skills. The shop was certainly no Dilbertian dystopia: management was not overtly evil, and everyone seemed matched with a job that more or less suited his ability. Those I knew were ready, willing, and able to put in a competent, honest day's work, though no one would pass up a sanctioned break. Some people showed infectious pride for workmanship, a certain joy in craftsmanship. Many had a keen sense of what was fair; you could almost sense the constant mental calculus. Admittedly, at least a couple had an eager-to-take-umbrage trade-unionist attitude. Though we were not a union shop, they did only exactly what was required by some secret or imaginary contract and constantly felt screwed.

Even if you weren't inclined to spring bright-eyed out of bed every morning, itching to print a few thousand Foxboro Company instruction sheets or parts lists, and even discounting what I likely missed due to naïveté and obliviousness and sheer lack of understanding, the print shop was not a bad place to work. Yet, to a man, when we talked about my studies—it was common knowledge that I was on summer vacation from college—my colleagues told me in so many words: work hard, do well in school, don't get trapped in a place like this, you can do better. Trapped? I didn't see it. They weren't printing hand-set limited edition poetry books on hand-made paper, but they had plenty of room to exercise technical competence, and I still harbored romantic notions of a life of honorable artisanship. They couldn't envision desktop publishing, the Internet, or that their printing jobs would be off-shored to China. But, after enduring years of work, they had glimpsed the limits of their world—and I had not.

Katey Schultz

Bare Bones: To Write, Draw

If you've ever stared blankly but lovingly at a small child's Crayola doodles across a piece of paper and said, "It's beautiful...*What is it?*" then you've probably also experienced the elated narrative explanation that comes next. Where you saw yellow squiggles, the young artist begins telling you about warm sunshine on a trip to the beach or the family's new golden retriever puppy that digs holes in the backyard and barks at turtles. Where you see stick figures, the child explains unique character traits, then adds emotional commentary about love, loss, promises for the future, or memories of the past.

It's no secret that these translations are a child's early attempts at story. To the child, yellow squiggles may as well be writing because at that stage letters and lines are both mere symbols used to convey meaning. What's striking is the fact that we leave this act of translation behind when we get older, as though we could somehow outgrow the value in this intuitive but profoundly influential cognitive process for relating story. As a fiction writer, I spend a good deal of time thinking about those cognitive processes—where do stories come from and why, how to get through a scene if I'm feeling stuck, and what makes one story leave an impression in my mind while another falls flat?

Which is why I was so moved by visual artist Philip Hartigan and author Patricia Ann McNair's presentation on the connections between writing and drawing at a conference this summer. Maybe it was the way the light angled through the mesh screens that afternoon, a hazy, softened yellow. Maybe it was the elated fatigue that sets in at the tail end of any such conference. Or maybe it was the fact that as guest faculty myself, Hartigan and McNair's presentation was my first moment to join the participants in an actual exercise all week. Either way, when they told me to stare out the window and slowly begin my first-ever blind contour drawing (*No peeking!*), I surrendered my I-can't-draw attitude and let intuition take over.

We worked quietly in our seats, completing a series of blind contour drawings as Hartigan and McNair asked us, gently, to keep drawing while calling to mind a particular scene from a story or line in a poem we felt stuck on. I thought immediately of a scene I'd been tinkering with to the point of boredom, wherein a quirky, antisocial main character named Tom stalks a neighborhood feline bully for several blocks in the middle of the night. We sketched for several more minutes, then Hartigan and McNair gave us permission to start writing. The catch? We could look at our notebooks as we wrote, but we had to cover up each line as we finished it—no going back, no perfectionist piddling, no previous sentence tarnishing whatever might come next.

Of course, unlike a child with Crayolas, I'm well aware of the difference between lines and letters. Hartigan and McNair's exercise wasn't as much about direct translation as it was about mimicking that feeling of carefree storytelling, whether consciously or not. But just because writers know how to use letters to convey meaning, doesn't mean we have to use them all the time. Furthermore, if we're writing a series of bland lines or paragraphs over and over, what makes us think that more writing is going to make it any better? Stories that make a meaningful impression to me—whether I'm reading a Pushcart Prize-winning author or a student's rough draft—are stories that present something fresh in terms of language and perspective. Writing outside the box requires thinking outside the box. To write better, write more, surely. But don't stop there. To write, *draw.*

Tom—my quirky, antisocial main character—ended up stalking the feline bully by army-crawling through a neighbor's garden and hiding out in a bed of ferns, much like a cat himself. And there, under the dim light of pre-dawn, he noticed drops of dew that reminded him of a pearl necklace his grandmother wore to her grave. His grandmother? Her grave? Where did *that* come from?

Exactly.

Contributor Biographies

Heather Clitheroe (Bacillus Anthracis) lives and works in Calgary. Her work can be found in the *Evolve* and *Awkard Two* anthologies, *Kaldeidotrope*, and *Hobart*. People sometimes describe her as a germaphobe. She feels she is simply germ aware, and would be happy to discuss the dangers of bean sprouts and unwashed hands. Try her. Go ahead. Try her.

Marianne Dages (Art) is a bookbinder and letterpress printer who lives and works in Philadelphia, Pennsylvania. She received her BFA in Photography from The University of the Arts in Philadelphia. In 2008, she was awarded the Core Fellowship at Penland School of Crafts in North Carolina where she studied printing, bookbinding, and papermaking for two years. She has been making books, prints, and other ephemera under the name Huldra Press since 2007. She is currently working on a variety of projects in her studio, including the restoration of a Chandler & Price printing press, which she documents on her blog, huldrapress.blogspot.com.

Pete Fromm (God's TV) is a four-time winner of the Pacific Northwest Booksellers Literary Award for his novels *As Cool As I Am* and *How All This Started*, a story collection, *Dry Rain*, and memoir, *Indian Creek Chronicles*. *As Cool As I Am* was filmed this summer, starring Claire Danes and Sarah Bolger, and will be released in 2012. He is the author of four other short story collections and also wrote the screenplay for the film adaptation of his short story, *Dry Rain*, and another original film, *After All This*. He is on the faculty of Oregon's Pacific University's Low-Residency MFA Program, and lives in Montana with his family.

Daniel Pinkerton (The Littlest Goat) lives with his family in Des Moines, Iowa. His fiction has appeared in *Quarterly West*, *Washington Square*, *Northwest Review*, *Arts & Letters*, *North American Review*, *Crazyhorse*, and the 2008 *Best New American Voices* anthology.

Ray Scanlon (Printer's Devil) was born, grew up, and lives in Massachusetts. He has grandchildren, extraordinary luck, and is pretty sure he could write a book, if only he had something to say. His web site is readoldmanscanlon.com.

TRACHODON: a dinosaur of a little magazine

Name_____

Address_____

City_____

State_____Zip_____

Email_____

[ ] 1-year subscription (2 issues) for $18.00
[ ] Single issue/sample copy for $10.00
Use our online system at www.trachodon.org or enclose a check payable to
Trachodon Publishing LLC and mail to:

TRACHODON
PO Box 1468
Saint Helens, OR 97051

TRACHODON: a dinosaur of a little magazine

Name_____

Address_____

City_____

State_____Zip_____

Email_____

[ ] 1-year subscription (2 issues) for $18.00
[ ] Single issue/sample copy for $10.00
Use our online system at www.trachodon.org or enclose a check payable to
Trachodon Publishing LLC and mail to:

TRACHODON
PO Box 1468
Saint Helens, OR 97051